marie claire
idées

Papercraft

Over 50 designs made with cut, folded, pasted and stitched paper

quadrille

This edition first published in 2009 by
Quadrille Publishing Limited
Alhambra House
27–31 Charing Cross Road
London WC2H 0LS

Original title: Créations en papier
© 2005 by Éditions MARIE CLAIRE–Société d'Information et de Créations (SIC)
10, boulevard des Frères-Voisin,
92130 Issy-Les-Moulineaux Cedex 9 – France

Translation and project management: Anne McDowall
Production Director: Vincent Smith
Production Controller: Denise Stone

British Library Cataloguing-in-Publication Data
A catalogue record for this book is available from the British Library.

ISBN: 978 184400 695 3

Printed in China

NOTES
Some of the templates have been reduced in scale. To find their correct size, enlarge them
on a photocopier until the scale bar on the template shows the measurement indicated.

Papercraft

Over 50 designs made with cut, folded, pasted and stitched paper

Contents

For the table

STARRY PLATES

MATERIALS
Sheets of white A4 writing paper ● Scissors ● Glass or clear plastic plates ● Tracing paper ● Spray glue.

METHOD
Cut out circles of paper of the same diameter as the plates. Fold each circle into 8. Enlarge the motifs on page 110 onto tracing paper so that they are of the same size as the folded paper circles. Trace the motifs onto one side of each of the folded paper cones, then cut out the designs carefully so that you are left with only the white areas. Unfold the paper decorations.

Working on a newspaper-covered surface and in a well-ventilated area, stick the paper decorations onto the underside of the plates using spray glue. Make sure that the smallest pieces are well secured so that they don't become unstuck and crinkled. (Note: these plates are purely decorative and cannot be placed in the dishwasher.)

(see also page 110)

For the table

CUTLERY MENU
Size: 24 x 12 cm

MATERIALS
**Card for the menus ● Scalpel ●
Metal ruler ● Coloured tracing
paper ● Indian ink and pen ●
Spray glue ● Buttons ● Glue stick
● Coloured thread.**

METHOD
Cut 24 cm squares of card for the
menus and fold them in half. Using
the ruler, tear along the vertical
edges of the card to create a raw
unfinished look. Cut rectangles of
tracing paper approximately 21 x
9 cm for the front of the menus.
Reduce the motifs opposite, then
place the tracing paper rectangles
on top and trace the design in
Indian ink.

Stick a tracing paper rectangle onto
the front of each menu card using
spray glue. Attach a button onto
the front of the menu using the glue
stick. Make a loop from coloured
thread and glue the ends onto the
back of the card, opposite the
button, to form a button loop.

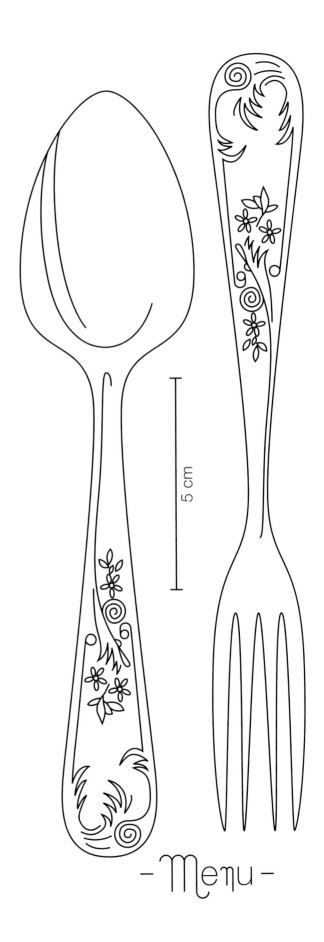

5 cm

– Menu –

- Menu -

For the table

NEWSPAPER DISHES

MATERIALS
Dishes (to serve as moulds) ●
Petroleum jelly ● Bowl ● White
glue ● Sheets of newspaper ●
Glue brush ● Scissors ● Grey
acrylic paint ● Paintbrush.

METHOD
Cover the inside of the mould with petroleum jelly. In a bowl, mix some white glue with water to thin it slightly. Tear the newspaper into small strips, coat them with glue, then stick them over the inside of the mould in an even layer. Leave to dry completely before applying the second layer. You will need at least 5 layers of paper for a firm dish. For a pleasing effect, use pieces of paper with the same size type for the final layer.

When the dish is completely dry, remove the mould and trim the edges of the dish with scissors. Paint a thin and a slightly thicker line around the inner edge using grey acrylic paint. The dried glue will form a protective varnish.

For the table

FAIRY TEA SERVICE

MATERIALS
Teapot and cup (to serve as moulds) ● Cling film ● Red and plum-coloured tissue paper ● Bowl ● White glue ● Glue brush ● Wire ● Strong glue (for attaching wire handles) ● Scalpel.

METHOD
Cover the teapot and cup with cling film, pulling it taut to avoid wrinkling. Tear the tissue paper into small pieces. In a bowl, mix some white glue with water to thin it slightly. Cover the pieces of tissue paper with glue and apply them to the cling film-covered surfaces using the glue brush.

Cup: Cover the outer surface of the cup with glued tissue paper. Leave to dry completely, then add another layer. Once this is dry, carefully remove the mould and the cling film. Cover the inside of the cup with pieces of glued paper, using the same technique, and leaving each layer to dry thoroughly before applying the next one, until the cup is firm enough.

Cut a length of wire, twist it into a handle and attach it to the side of the cup using strong glue.

Teapot: Cover the whole surface of the teapot with pieces of glued tissue paper. Leave to dry, then apply a second layer.
Once this is completely dry, carefully split open the papier mâché casing, from top to bottom and through the spout, using a scalpel, to remove the teapot. Place the 2 halves side by side and join them together with a layer of glued paper overlapping the 2 halves.
Finish by making and attaching a wire handle, as for the cup.

For the table

WINDOW AND CAKE GARLANDS

WINDOW GARLAND

MATERIALS
**4 sheets of A4 tracing paper ●
Masking tape ● Pencil ● Scalpel ●
Card punch ● Cutting mat ● 60 x
50 cm of tarlatan ● Scissors ●
String ● Glue.**

METHOD
Enlarge each of the letter motifs on
page 111 to fit on the A4 sheet and
attach each to a sheet of tracing
paper using masking tape. Lightly
trace the design onto the tracing
paper, then remove the template.
Cut out the centre of the letters and
the other elements in the design.
Cut pieces of tarlatan slightly smaller
than A4 size and stick them behind
each 'empty space'.
Cut the string to the required length
of the garland and centre the letters
along it, spacing them about 10 cm
apart. Attach them in place by
folding the top edge over the string
and gluing in place.

CAKE GARLAND

MATERIALS
**Bristol board ● Masking tape ●
Scalpel ● Cutting mat.**

METHOD
Enlarge the template on page 111
(the size given is for a 12–14 cm-
diameter cake) and attach it to the
Bristol board with masking tape.
Cut out the outline using a scalpel
and cut open the slits. Fold up the
edges and slot the tabs into the slits
as shown on the template.
You can experiment with different
sizes of tins and by varying the
decoration of the edge.

(see also page 111)

For the table

NOSTALGIA IN GLASS

MATERIALS
Antique glass flycatcher or other glass vessel with a wide mouth ● Flower and foliage découpage motifs ● Nail scissors ● Découpage glue ● Soft cloth ● Clear varnish ● Flexible paintbrush for the varnish ● Fine paintbrush for the paint ● Gloss paint.

1. Carefully cut out the chosen découpage motifs, reserving the more compact flower and foliage pieces for the base of the glass.

2. Coat the printed sides of the designs with glue. Stick them firmly on the interior surface of the jar and press with a soft cloth to remove all air bubbles. Leave to dry.

3. Using a flexible paintbrush, paint over the edges of the designs with a varnish to waterproof the surface. Leave to dry.

4. To finish, fill in the background with gloss paint, using a fine paintbrush, making sure to trace carefully around the motifs.

For the table

LACY MENUS

MATERIALS
Decorative paints ● Paintbrush ● White or coloured cards ● White and gold paper doilies ● Spray glue ● Gold pen ● Scissors ● Tracing paper ● Gold metallic elastic cord.

METHOD
Paint the cards and/or the doilies. Leave to dry.
Cover the cards with the doilies, inside and out, matching or contrasting colours. Use spray glue to stick the doilies in place, folding over excess onto the other side of the card.
Use a gold pen to highlight details of the doily pattern and to write 'menu' at the top of each card.
Cut a sheet of tracing paper to the dimensions of the open card, fold in half, and slip it inside the card.
Tie a length of gold elastic cord in place around the spine to hold the menu in place.

For the table

TIERED TRAY
Size: 50 x 46 cm

MATERIALS
3 squares of 5mm-thick plywood: 45 cm², 31 cm² and 18 cm² ● 1 cm² wooden lath: 4 lengths of 52 cm, 4 lengths of 43 cm, 4 lengths of 29 cm and 4 lengths of 16 cm ● Saw ● Wood glue ● Hammer ● 20 mm-wide panel pins ● Pencil ● Coloured tissue paper ● Scissors ● Red and white acrylic paints.

METHOD
Following the diagram opposite, make 2 ladders, joining the lengths of wooden lath together using wood glue and panel pins. Leave to dry. Join the remaining lengths of lath onto 2 top opposite edges of each plywood square using wood glue and panel pins. Leave to dry.

Assemble the 2 ladders and 3 trays, gluing and nailing the crosspieces of the ladders to the top of opposite sides of each tray (You will need to cut in to the crosspieces to match them up with the uprights.) Leave to dry.

Paint the whole structure using white acrylic paint, then, when dry,

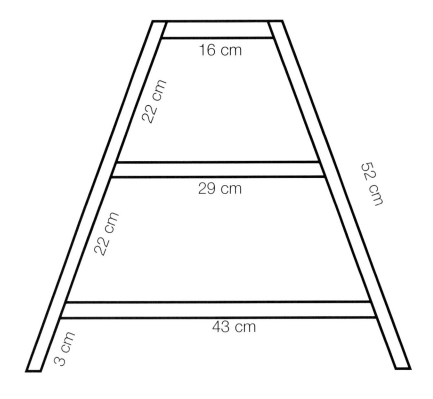

with red acrylic paint. Copy a mosaic design from a book, or make up your own, and draw it lightly onto the tray. Cut out small shapes from

tissue paper and stick them onto the design with diluted wood glue, leaving a gap of about 5 mm between the pieces. Leave to dry.

For the table

DAILY PAPERS

MATERIALS
Table and chairs ● Wallpaper paste ● Bowl ● A large quantity of newspaper ● Paintbrushes ● Wallpaper paste brush ● Matt varnish.

METHOD
Clean the table and chairs to remove any traces of dust or grease that would prevent the newspaper from sticking to them.

Prepare the wallpaper paste in a bowl, following the manufacturer's instructions.

Wet newspaper is fragile to handle, so it is best to work on a small area at a time. Cover the surface to be papered with wallpaper paste, lay a piece of newspaper onto it, and use a paintbrush, coated with more wallpaper paste, to fix it in place.

Use a wallpaper brush to dab the paper around the curves and edges of the table and chairs, making sure that it is pressed into all the corners. Depending on the effect you are wanting to achieve, you can cover each piece of furniture with a single layer of paper or with several, but leave each one to dry before applying the next. Avoid papering the edges of drawers, otherwise the thickness of paper might prevent them from opening, and ensure that the table top is completely flat so that anything you place on it remains stable.

Once the final layer is completely dry, make sure that there are no loose corners of paper peeling up, then apply 2 coats of matt varnish to protect the surfaces.

For the table

ORIGAMI POCKETS

MATERIALS
Coloured card: squares of 20, 25, 35 and 45 cm ● 25 cm length of ribbon for each holder ● Tapestry needle ● Gel glue.

METHOD
All these 'pockets' are folded in the same way, by marking the folds with your nail at each stage.

Following the diagrams on page 112, fold each square in 4 to mark the centre point, then open out again (1). Fold over each corner to the centre point (2 and 3). Turn the card over and mark the centre as in step 1 (4). Fold the new corners into the centre (5). Fold this square in half, from top to bottom (6).

Slide the thumb and index finger of your right hand underneath the righthand corners of the fold (thumb in front, index finger behind); slide the thumb and index finger of your left hand under the lefthand points. Open the pockets by bringing the 4 points to the centre. Remove your fingers and thumbs and turn the shape over so that it rests on these 4 points.

Pierce the centre of each origami shape and, using the needle, thread through a length of ribbon so that the ends are on the wrong side. Knot the ends and fix them in place with a dab of glue.

Fill the pockets with rose petals, little pebbles, sweets, salt or pepper...

(see also page 112)

Vases and flowers

TALL RED VASES

MATERIALS
Muslin ● Iron-on interfacing ●
Scissors ● Needle ● Sewing
thread ● Bowl ● White glue ●
Glue brush ● Red tissue paper
and/or Chinese paper.

METHOD
In the muslin and interfacing, cut a
10.5 cm-diameter circle and a
rectangle of 33 cm x the desired
height of the vase, adding a 1 cm
seam allowance around all sides.
Iron the interfacing onto each piece.
Make the rectangle into a tube by
sewing together the 2 heights, right
sides together, then sew the tube
around the circle. Turn right side out.
In a bowl, mix some white glue with
water to thin it slightly. Tear the
tissue paper and/or Chinese paper
into small pieces. Coat the paper
with glue and apply it to the tube,
working from the bottom up. Allow
each layer to dry before applying
the next one. When the final layer is
completely dry, even up the top
edge with scissors.

Vases and flowers

WEDDING POSY

MATERIALS
White, lilac and pale green tissue paper ● Scissors ● Thick white cotton thread ● Toothpicks.

METHOD
For each flower stem, cut an 80 x 2 cm strip of green tissue paper and an 80 cm length of cotton thread. Lay the thread along one long edge of the paper and, with wet fingers, roll the paper around it. Leave to dry. For each petal, cut a 20 x 5 cm strip of tissue paper. Lay a toothpick at an angle across one of the short edges (see opposite), then roll the paper around it until you reach the centre. Do the same from the other top corner. Carefully remove the toothpicks. Prepare other petals in the same way. To make different sizes of flower, allow between 5 and 20 petals for each one.

Curl one end of a dried stem to form a stamen, then lay it across the base of a petal so it overlaps the petal edge by about 6 cm. With wet fingers, roll the base of the petal around the stem. Fix all the petals to the stem in the same way.

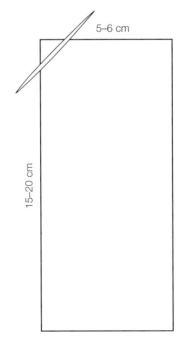

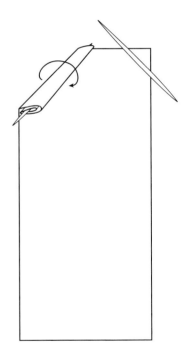

Vases and flowers

EXOTIC STAMP VASE

MATERIALS

A large quantity of floral stamps (or printouts or photocopies of stamp motifs) ● Vase ● Strong glue ● Glue brush ● Yellow and sepia ink ● Paintbrushes (for inks and varnish) ● Ageing varnish.

METHOD

Sort the stamps according to their format so that you can easily select the best ones to use on different parts of the vase. Stick them to the vase with strong glue, overlapping them so that none of the vase can be seen. Leave to dry.

Mix the inks in equal quantities and paint over the stamps. Leave to dry, then paint the vase with ageing varnish to protect and antiquate it.

Vases and flowers

FLOWER BAG

MATERIALS

Strong card gift bag ● Sharp pencil ● Sewing machine ● Coloured sewing thread ● Paper glue ● Thin wire ● Small coloured beads ● Card punch ● Cutting mat ● 4 eyelets, 5 mm-wide ● Eyelet setter ● Hammer.

METHOD

Remove the handles from the bag and carefully unglue the seams so that you can lay it flat.

Draw the design onto the bag with a pencil. Thread the sewing machine with coloured thread and machine-stitch over the design using a satin stitch of width 2/3 and length 0.5. Reassemble the bag, gluing the seams with paper glue.

Cut a length of thin wire for each handle and thread the beads onto these wires.

Make 2 holes on each side of the bag, spacing them equidistant from each side. Push the eyelet through the punched-out hole so that the decorative side of the eyelet faces down towards the cutting mat, with the fastener side facing up towards you. Place the tip of the eyelet setter into the centre of the fastener. With a hammer, tap the top of the eyelet setter. Remove the eyelet setter. Using the hammer, tap down the edges of the fastener to flatten to the bag.

Slip the ends of one handle into the 2 holes in the front of the bag, the ends of the other handle into those in the back. Twist the ends on the wrong side to secure the handles in place. Reshape the handles.

Vases and flowers

FOLDED PAPER VASES

MATERIALS
Stiff card ● Scissors ● Cylindrical vase ● Pencil ● Ruler ● Round coffee filter papers ● Sewing machine ● White sewing thread ● Strong glue.

METHOD
Cut a rectangle of card to cover the vase, allowing an extra strip for the overlap. Using the pencil and ruler, divide the rectangle into horizontal bands the same height as the diameter of the filter papers. Then draw vertical lines 1 cm apart, staggering the rows from one horizontal band to the next.

Fold the filter papers in half and stitch them onto the card, placing the centre fold of a filter paper against each of the vertical pencil lines, to completely cover the surface of the card.

Wrap the card around the vase and glue in place.

Vases and flowers

POTS OF FLOWERS

MATERIALS
Compost pots ● White acrylic paint ● Paintbrush ● Thin wire ● Pliers ● Scissors ● Tissue paper: pink, white, mauve, red ● All-purpose glue.

METHOD
Paint the compost pots with a thin layer of white acrylic paint.

For each of the small roses and rosebuds, cut a 25 cm length of wire. Fold the wire in half and twist the ends together, leaving a small loop at the centre.

For each of the large roses, cut a 50 cm length of wire. Leaving 12 cm at each end, twist the central part to make about 10 heart-shaped petals of different sizes, their bases all joining in the centre. Twist the ends of the wire together.

Cut hearts of various sizes from the tissue paper. Paint one side of each heart white, experimenting with different intensities of colour.

For the small roses, glue a petal to each side of the wire loop, then glue the bases of 10 others all around the twisted-wire stem.

For the large roses, group petals all around the stem and between the wire petals, gluing their bases to the twisted wire.

Arrange the flowers in the compost pots, mixing up the sizes and colours, then place the pots down the centre of the table.

Vases and flowers

PAPIER MÂCHÉ JUGS

MATERIALS

Brass wire ● Wire cutters ● 25 mm-diameter wire mesh ● Flat-nosed pliers ● Bowl ● Large quantity of newspaper ● White and coloured acrylic paints ● Paintbrushes.

METHOD

You will need to build a wire structure for each of the jugs. Using the brass wire, form a ring for the base, one for the top – adding a lip – and several intermediate ones. Working from the bottom to the top, join the rings together with at least 8 vertical wires, attaching the latter to the rings with knots of brass wire. Add handles, and spouts to the jug forms, and construct the shape for the teapot lid, as desired.

To create an armature (the skeleton), wrap the mesh over the structural frame. Fold in edges over the wire structure and tie with brass wires as needed.

Tear the newspaper into strips, and prepare the wallpaper paste in a bowl, following the manufacturer's instructions. Coat the newspaper strips with wallpaper paste, then lay them onto the structure, overlapping them slightly to cover the whole surface. Leave to dry. Add several layers, leaving each to dry before applying the next, until the shapes are generously covered and suitably robust.

Apply several coats of white paint to the jugs to give a uniform colour, leave to dry, then paint each in coordinating or contrasting colours of your choice.

Vases and flowers

ARUM-LILY CORONET

MATERIALS
Tracing paper ● Pencil ● White paper ● Scissors ● Sheets of newspaper ● Paper glue ● Paintbrushes ● Acrylic paints: white, golden yellow, pistachio green and pale spring green ● Hairdryer ● Wallpaper paste ● Bowl ● 5.60 m of 2.5 mm-diameter wire ● Cutting pliers ● Nylon thread ● Needle.

METHOD
Trace the motifs on page 113 and cut them out to make a template. Cut out 9 flowers and 12 leaves in the white paper.

Cut a 10 x 5 cm strip of newspaper for each flower and leaf. Roll up each strip tightly from the short side, securing at the end with a line of glue, to make a 5 cm-long stick.

Roll the leaves and flowers around these 'stamens' as shown in the diagrams on page 113, securing them in place by gluing a little ring of paper tightly around the base.

Paint the flowers and leaves with at least 5 coats of white paint, drying them with a hairdryer between each one. (These layers of paint will help to solidify the elements.) Paint the leaves in the shades of green and the stamens in golden yellow. Leave to dry.

Tear the remaining newspaper into strips and prepare the wallpaper paste in a bowl, following the manufacturer's instructions. Coat the newspaper strips with wallpaper paste and wrap them tightly around the wire. Leave to dry.

Paint with white acrylic paint, then, when dry, with green. Curl the wire into a coronet about 60 cm in diameter. To complete the coronet, sew the leaves and flowers onto it using the nylon thread.

(see also page 113)

Vases and flowers

BOUQUET OF FLOWERS

MATERIALS
Pencil ● Compass ● White tissue paper ● Scissors ● Thin wire ● Round black sticky labels.

METHOD
Using a pencil, and a compass if necessary, trace the circles on page 114 directly onto sheets of white tissue paper, lightly marking the parts to be cut out – shown in grey on the template. (Alternatively, you can simply draw circles of approximately 9 cm diameter and cut out different designs freehand.) Cut out the circles, fold in half, then in half again, then into 3, keeping the segment with the design drawn on it on top. Cutting through all layers of paper at once, remove the marked parts of the design. Open out the circles.

Cut the flower stems from the thin wire and poke one end through the centre of each flower, from back to front. Bend over the wire end and stick a black label on top to hide it and form the flower centre.

(see also page 114)

Lights

PUNCHED HOLES

DECORATIVE VOTIVES

MATERIALS
Glass tumblers ● Scrap paper
● Handmade paper ● Scissors
● Bradawl or large needle ●
Strong glue.

METHOD
Wrap a tumbler in a piece of paper to obtain its dimensions. Transfer the shape to a sheet of handmade paper, allowing an extra strip for the overlap. Cut out this pattern.

Enlarge the motifs on page 115 on a photocopier so that they fit the size of the tumblers. Place them on the paper and, working on a protected surface, punch the holes using a bradawl or large needle. Glue the hole-punched paper around the glass.

Take inspiration from these 3 motifs and design your own decorative ones. (Search through cross-stitch books to discover lots of frieze and festive design ideas.)

SMALL DISHES

MATERIALS
Sheets of newspaper ● Bowl ●
Electric mixer ● 2 sieves of the same size ● White and gold acrylic paint ● 1 large and 1 medium paintbrush.

METHOD
Tear the newspaper into tiny pieces and leave to soak overnight in a bowl of water. Squeeze out excess water, then blend the soaked paper in the mixer to form a thick pulp.

Spread around the base and sides of one of the sieves to a thickness of about 5 mm. Press the other sieve inside and leave to dry.

Remove the hardened dish from the mould and paint the inside and outside using white acrylic paint. Paint the rim of the dish gold.

(see also page 115)

Lights

PAPER PUMPKINS

MATERIALS
Newspaper ● Garland of white Japanese lanterns ● Coloured stickers: 2 sizes of round stickers and 2 sizes of stars ● Rubber gloves ● Orange spray paint ● Reel of wire ● Wire cutters ● Japanese paper: 1 sheet of dark green and 1 sheet of medium green ● Pencil ● Spray glue ● Eraser ● Scissors.

METHOD
Make sure that your work space is well ventilated but draught free, and that you cover your work surface with plenty of newspaper.

Re-form the lanterns, remove them from the garland and decorate with stickers. Wearing rubber gloves, cover the lanterns with a light but even coat of orange spray paint. Leave to dry, then spray with a second coat to ensure that the colour is as uniform as possible.

Cut some 7.5 cm lengths of wire. Apply glue to one side of the medium-green paper and wrap the paper around the wires. Twist the wires around a finger or a pencil to form tendrils.

Trace the leaf shape below and transfer it to the dark-green paper. Tear or cut out several leaves. Spray glue to the bottom of the strips and attach them to the wire stems.

When the painted lanterns are completely dry, carefully remove the stickers. Attach the wire stems to the structure of the lanterns, then reattach these to the garland.

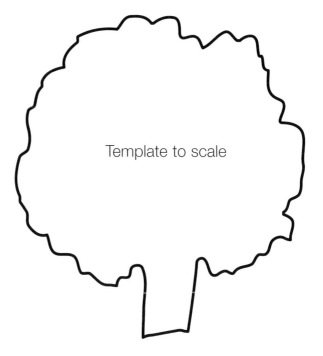

Template to scale

Lights

BAROQUE LAMPSHADE

MATERIALS

2 sheets of textured white card, each 102 x 70 cm ● Pencil ● Ruler ● Scalpel ● Lampshade frame: 25/30 cm in diameter, 29 cm high ● Glue gun .

METHOD

Cut the card into 70 x 3 cm strips. Curl one end to 20 cm of its length. Turn the strip over and repeat with the other end.

Position the curled strips on the lampshade frame by folding them over the top rim by varying amounts to give strips of different lengths, some with curls facing outwards, with others facing inwards. Glue them in position using the glue gun. If necessary, you can fill any gaps with strips that have been rolled at only one end.

Lights

FLORAL SHADES

MATERIALS

**White and orange recycled paper
● Scissors ● Paper glue ● Scalpel
● Cutting mat ● Pencil or
coloured crayons ● Eraser ●
5 mm-diameter balsa-wood rods
● Long wooden skewers.**

METHOD

Cut squares or rectangles of paper
of adequate size to screen your
chosen lights.

Draw daisies on the paper with the
pencil or coloured crayons (the latter
if you want to retain these marks
as part of the design). Carefully cut
out certain parts of the flowers
using the scalpel.

For a flat screen (as top right), cut
the balsa-wood rods to the lengths
of the sides and glue to the edges
on the back to form a frame.

To make the curved screens, pierce
the middle of each side edge with a
wooden skewer that is shorter than
the width of the paper. Secure with
dabs of glue on the inside. (If the
screen is large, use 2 skewers
across the top and bottom.)

Lights

SUMMER LANTERN

MATERIALS
White decorative paper ● Straight-sided glass vase ● Scissors ● Scalpel ● Relief paint and paintbrush (optional, see method) ● Hairdryer (optional, see method) ● Strong glue ● Pencil ● White handmade paper ● Thin twig ● String of fairy lights.

METHOD
Cut a rectangle of the decorative paper the height of your vase and long enough to encircle it, allowing for an overlap to glue it in place.

The design of the paper used for this lantern has holes with raised edges. If you are unable to find something similar, cut out irregular circles over the whole surface using a scalpel and paint a fine line of relief paint around each hole. Dry the paint with a hairdryer to puff up the paint.

Stick the paper around the vase with a line of glue on the overlapping edge.

Draw a large butterfly freehand on the white handmade paper and cut out. Stick it onto the top of the twig, then slide the other end of the twig through a hole in the lantern.

Feed the fairy lights into the vase, hiding the lead at the back.

Lights

NEWSPRINT LANTERNS

Sizes: 15 x 10 cm and 20 x 15 cm

MATERIALS

3 mm-thick cardboard (see method for dimensions) ● Scalpel ● 1 cm-square wooden rod (allow 1 m length for small lantern and 1.5 m for large one) ● Pencil ● Ruler ● Saw ● Glue gun ● Old foreign newspapers ● Scissors ● Tealights.

METHOD

For the small lantern, cut a 10 cm square of the 3 mm-thick cardboard to form the base. Cut 4 lengths of wooden rod of 15 cm to form the uprights of the structure. Using the glue gun, glue the ends to each of the corners of the base.

Cut 4 lengths of rod of 8 cm and glue them between the uprights at the top to strengthen and complete the structure.

Once the glue is completely dry, cover the structure with strips of newspaper, either using one large piece and wrapping and gluing it tightly around the whole structure, or covering each side with a rectangle of paper. Leave to dry.

Make the large lantern in the same way, using a 15 cm cardboard square for the base, 20 cm lengths of rod for the uprights and 15 cm-long rods for the top of the frame. Place a tealight into the bottom of each of the lanterns.

Lights

CANDELABRA

Size: 58 x 84 cm

MATERIALS

3 mm-thick greyboard: 2 sheets of 120 x 80 cm ● Scissors ● Scalpel ● Protractor ● Pencil ● White glue ● Elastic band ● Rope ● Tarlatan ● Newspaper ● Bowl ● Wallpaper paste ● Tissue paper ● Paintbrushes ● Grey acrylic paint ● Thick long needle ● Wire ● Wire cutters ● 6 tealights .

METHOD

Enlarge the template on page 116 and, using a scalpel, cut out 6 candelabra shapes with arms and 6 without (following the dotted line) from the greyboard. Cut out a 23 cm-diameter circle for the base of the candelabra. On the base of this circle, draw 6 diameters to divide it into 12 segments of equal size. Draw a line of white glue along each radius of the circle, then place the bottom edge of the candelabra shapes onto them, alternating shapes with and without arms, so that the shapes all join in the centre. Hold the shapes together while the glue dries with an elastic band around the body of the candelabra. Cut 12 reinforcing pieces – shown in grey on the template – from the greyboard. Stick them on both sides of each arm. Cut out 36 half-candle-ring shapes and 6 circles of 10 cm in diameter. Stick the flat sides of 3 half-candle-ring shapes to each side of the candle-ring at the end of each arm, spacing them at equal angles apart. Stick a card circle on top of each candle-ring. Knot one end of the rope and lay it so the knot lies just below the neck and between two segments of the candelabra. Carefully tape the rope to each side of the segment for added security.

Cut strips of tarlatan about 3 cm wide and wrap them around the candelabra, fixing them in place with a few spots of glue.

In a bowl, mix up the wallpaper paste, following the manufacturer's instructions. Tear up the newspaper into strips, soak in the wallpaper paste, and apply to the candelabra shape. Allow each layer to dry before applying the next one. Finish with a layer of tissue paper. Once the candelabra is completely dry, paint it using grey acrylic paint. Place a tealight on each candle-ring and suspend the candelabra from the ceiling with the rope.

(see also page 116)

Lights

FEATHERED PAPER LANTERN

MATERIALS

White and pink acrylic paints ● Small jars or plastic cups for mixing paint ● Paper lantern ● Paintbrush ● White glue ● Pink feathers.

METHOD

Put some white acrylic paint in each of several jars or cups. Add some pink paint to each cup, varying the amount added to each cup to give different shades of pink.

Paint each section of the paper lampshade in a different shade of pink. (Note: the paint will need to be relatively thick to prevent it soaking the paper.) Leave to dry.

Glue the feathers onto the lampshade in a random pattern.

Lights

CHINESE LANTERNS
Size: 30 x 20 cm

MATERIALS
Transparent sticky-back plastic (you will need an 84 x 30 cm rectangle for each lantern) ● Ruler ● Pencil ● Scissors ● Tissue paper in various bright colours ● Scalpel ● Thin wooden rod (you will need a 1.6 m length for each rectangular lantern) ● Rubber cement ● 20 cm-diameter wire lampshade frame ● Thin wire ● Needle ● Coloured paper ● Spray glue.

METHOD
Cut an 84 x 30 cm rectangle from the transparent sticky-back plastic. Mark 1 cm in from both sides of the long edge. Between these 2 points, mark 3 lines at 20 cm intervals along the length for the lantern corners (see the diagram on page 117). Remove the backing paper and carefully lay tissue paper over the surface, leaving 1 cm at each short edge clear. Press in place. Cut 8 lengths of wooden rod of 19.5 cm and glue them along each long side, as shown on page 117, using rubber cement. Form the lantern by sticking the two short edges together on the inside.

Slip the lampshade frame into the top of the lantern. Secure it in position with several stitches of wire through the plastic.

Cut out various motifs – starfish, shells or birds, for example – from the coloured paper. Stick them onto each side of the lantern using the spray glue.

Make various lanterns in the same way, varying the colours, decoration and dimensions as desired (making sure that you can find lampshade frames of a suitable size to fit).

(see also page 117)

Lights

TEALIGHT HOLDERS

MATERIALS

**4 small straight-sided glass jars ●
Japanese handmade paper ●
Scissors ● 3D craft paint ● Letter
stencils ● Stencil brush ● Paper
glue ● 4 tealights.**

METHOD

Cut out 4 strips from the Japanese
paper the height of the jars and long
enough to encircle the them and
allow for an overlap of 2 cm.

Lay a letter stencil in the middle of
each paper strip and apply the 3D
craft paint using a stencil brush.
Leave the paint to dry before
removing the stencil.

Close the bands with a few dabs
of glue along the edge. Slip them
over the glass jars and place a
tealight in each one. (As a safety
precaution, make sure that the
paper band is no higher than the
top of the jars.)

Gift wrapping

QUILLED-PAPER BOXES

MATERIALS

White card boxes with lids ● Decorative paints ● Small paint roller ● Thick paper of different colours ● Scalpel ● Small metal ruler ● All-purpose glue ● Knitting needle or pencil ● Cocktail stick ● Tweezers.

METHOD

Paint the outside of each box and its lid, using the roller, with 2 coats of paint, leaving the paint to dry after each coat.

Cut strips of coloured paper 2, 3 or 5 mm wide. For the linear motifs, such as the letters or flower stems shown opposite, design the chosen shapes onto the box using a pencil or end of a knitting needle. Use a cocktail stick to trace a line of glue in the channel thus formed, then carefully place the paper strips into position, laying them flat or on their sides, depending on the effect desired.

Shape relief motifs, such as the clovers and hearts, from the paper strips by rolling the ends around the knitting needle to create scrolls.

Using the cocktail stick, carefully draw a line of glue along the edge of the curled strips and place them into position on the boxes, holding them in place for a minute with your finger. You can use tweezers to handle the smallest motifs.

Gift wrapping

FANTASTICAL BOXES

MATERIALS

Old boxes ● An assortment of coloured papers: sweet wrappers, paper doilies, foreign packaging, stickers, papers with different textures, shredded tissue paper ● Paper glue ● Gloss medium or clear varnish ● Paintbrush.

METHOD

Cover the boxes in different papers, overlapping them to cover all surfaces. Smooth out bubbles and wrinkles using your thumb, being careful not to rip the paper. Apply 3 or 4 coats of gloss medium or clear varnish to the finished surface after it has completely dried. Allow the surface to dry between coats.

Alternatively, wrap a box in coloured paper, then attach pieces of other papers or stickers.

The wild box in the top left corner of the picture is covered with strips of tissue paper that have been passed through a paper shredder.

Gift wrapping

CUT-PAPER COVERINGS

MATERIALS
Large sheets of thick white paper
● Cutting mat ● Pencil ● Scalpel
● Paper glue ● Coloured tissue
paper ● Textured white wallpaper
● Foreign newspapers.

METHOD
To make the paper cornet, spread out a sheet of paper on the cutting mat. Sketch motifs in pencil onto the paper: draw the geometric motifs on the wrong side, any text or letters on the right side. Carefully cut out the shapes using the scalpel. Roll the paper into a cone shape, fixing it in place with a dab of glue. Slip a sheet of coloured tissue paper inside the paper cornet to highlight the cut-out motifs.

To make the relief flowers, cut a piece of the textured white paper large enough to wrap the present. Mark the part that will cover the top of the parcel. Working slowly and carefully, cut the outline of flower shapes, making sure that you always leave a part to attach the flower to the paper. Wrap up the present in the paper, then, using a scalpel, carefully lift the cut pieces away from the rest.

To make the tousled flowers, cut a long strip of white paper or foreign newpaper. Draw a line 1 cm in from the edge along the length of this strip, then cut from the edge to this line every 5 or 10 mm. Roll up the strip and fix the loose end with a dab of glue. Stick it onto the parcel, then separate the 'petals'.

Gift wrapping

MONEY-COVERED BOXES

MATERIALS

1 wooden wine crate (with lid) and 1 tea caddy ● A large quantity of bank notes and coins ● Sandpaper ● Spray glue ● Scalpel ● Self-adhesive aluminium foil ● Hammer ● Upholstery nails ● Gloss medium or clear varnish ● Paintbrush ● 2 hinges (with 4 small screws for each) ● Small screwdriver ● Glue gun ● Drawing pins.

METHOD

To make the note-covered chest, clean and lightly sand the box to remove any splinters that could pierce the notes.

Working on one side of the box at a time, spray the whole surface with glue, then stick the bank notes in position, overlapping them so that the whole side is covered. Smooth out bubbles and wrinkles in the notes using your thumb, being careful not to rip the notes. Spray underneath any overlapping edges so that they do not curl up.

Cut the self-adhesive aluminium foil into strips long enough to cover each edge of the box. Fold 8 of them at right angles and use these to cover the bottom and side edges. Fold the remaining strips around the top edges of the box and the edges of the lid.

Apply 3 or 4 coats of gloss medium or clear varnish to the finished surface after it has completely dried. Allow the surface to dry between coats.

Hammer upholstery nails around the edges at regular intervals.

Screw the hinges into position to attach the lid to the box.

To make the coin-covered box, attach strips of self-adhesive foil to the edges of the box and lid and hammer in upholstery nails, following the instructions given for the note-covered chest.

Working on one side of the box at a time, line up an assortment of coins in rows to cover the surface. Stick them in position using the glue gun. You can attach drilled coins with a drawing pin through the centre but be careful that the pins don't pass through to the inside of the box. If the box sides are too thin, stick the drilled coins to the surface, then either glue the head of a pin on top or leave the hole visible.

Gift wrapping

PAINTED GIFT BAGS

MATERIALS
**White kraft paper ● Scissors ●
Ruler ● Pencil ● Large and small
paintbrushes ● Bowls ● Silk paint
in various colours ● 3D craft paint
● Double-sided tape ● Scalpel ●
Ribbon.**

Method
Cut a rectangle of paper to the
dimensions shown on the template
on page 118.

Lay the paper flat and paint with
silk paint diluted with water. Leave
to dry flat to prevent it distorting.

Draw a motif on what will become
the front panel of the bag, then
paint it with the 3D craft paint
following the manufacturer's
instructions. Leave to dry.

Mark all the the folds of the bag –
all should be in relief except the
central fold on the side gussets,
which should be folded inwards.
Close the bag at the back with a
strip of double-sided tape. Fold the
bottom of the bag and close with
double-sided tape.

Pinch the front and back of the bag
together at the top and fold over
twice, by 3 cm each time. Using
the scalpel, cut 2 parallel vertical
slits in the centre of the top of the
bag, cutting through all the layers.
Slide a length of decorative ribbon
through the slits and tie it in a bow
at the front of the bag.

(see also page 118)

Gift wrapping

MINI SILVER BOXES

MATERIALS
Aluminium foil ● Scissors ● Small metal cake tins ● Beads, fake gems, ribbon ● Strong glue.

METHOD
Cut the aluminium foil into small pieces of matching size. Lay them on top of each other until you have a thickness that holds its shape well but is still pliable (the number of layers you need will depend on the quality of the foil used).

To create the outside of the gift box, cover the outside of the cake tin with these pieces of foil, ensuring that layers adhere to each other. The overlapping of the pieces will give the finished box substance. Cut off any edges of foil that are overhanging the top of the tin, then remove the tin.

Repeat the above steps, this time layering the foil pieces inside the tin, to create the inside of the box. To finish, glue a bead, fake gem or length of ribbon to the bottom of the inside box.

Gift wrapping

LEAFY ENVELOPES

MATERIALS

White tissue paper ● Brown wrapping paper ● Scissors ● Craft glue ● Card punch ● Twigs ● Leaves ● White spray paint ● Sheets of scrap paper.

METHOD

Wrap up a present in white tissue paper. Cut a piece of brown wrapping paper with a 5 cm overlap so that it is large enough to easily enclose the parcel when it is folded in half.

Depending on the size of the parcel, stick 2 or 3 sides together with a line of glue. To close remaining sides, punch 2 holes and thread a twig through them.

To decorate the parcel, cover some leaves with white spray paint, leave to dry, and stick onto the parcel. Alternatively, place some sheets of paper over the ends of the parcel and lay the leaves over the middle section, then spray with paint. Carefully remove the leaves.

Gift wrapping

STATIONERY BAGS
Size: 21 x 13.5 cm

MATERIALS

Large sheets of handwritten paper, ideally aged; if necessary, enlarged on a photocopier ● Medium-thickness iron-on fabric stiffener (the same dimensions as the sheets of paper) ● Ruler ● Pencil ● Scissors ● Sewing machine ● Sewing thread ● Pins.

METHOD

Iron the fabric stiffener to the back of the sheets of paper. Following the template on page 119, draw the shape of the bag and the 2 handles on the back, and cut them out.

Form the bag by folding up the sides, with wrong sides facing, and machine-stitch them together, 3 mm in from the edges. Stitch all around the base of the bag to define the edges.

Stitch along the lengths of the handles, 3 mm from the edges. Pin the ends of one handle inside the bag, approximately 9 cm apart and equidistant from the sides. Repeat with the other handle on the opposite side. Stitch around the top of the bag, catching the handles into the seam. Remove pins.

To make the bag charms, cut long strips of paper and, with wet fingers, roll them around lengths of cotton thread. Cut out 2 hearts from the handwritten paper and 2 from the fabric stiffener. Lay them on top of each other, slip the end of a twisted paper ribbon between the 2, then iron to fix the layers together and trap the ribbon.

(see also page 119)

Christmas

ORIENTAL LIDDED BOWLS

MATERIALS

Bowl ● Wallpaper paste ● 2 small round balloons ● String ● Scissors ● 2 sheets of red paper of A3 format ● Newspaper ● Pin ● Tape measure ● Pencil ● Scalpel ● Corrugated card (1.5 cm-wide strip the length of the perimeter of the papier mâché balloon for each bowl, plus a 6 cm-diameter circle for the small bowl) ● Strong glue ● Gold-coloured wire ● Wire cutters ● Copper-coloured relief pen ● 2 decorative beads.

METHOD

In a bowl, prepare the wallpaper paste, following the manufacturer's instructions. Leave to rest for 10 minutes. Blow up the 2 balloons, knot the ends and tie a piece of string to each from which to suspend them.

Tear the red paper into small pieces. Soak them in the wallpaper paste and then stick them to the balloons until each is covered. Leave to dry overnight.

Repeat, this time using newspaper. Apply a total of 6 or 7 layers of newspaper, allowing each of the first 3 coats to dry before applying the next. Successive layers can be applied 2 at a time. Leave to dry. Finish with a final layer of red paper. Leave to dry again.

Burst the balloon by sticking a pin into the top. Measure the papier mâché balloon to find the centre, then draw a straight line in pencil all around the middle. Cut the shape open along this line, using a scalpel. Remove the burst balloon. For the large bowl, cut a strip of corrugated card 1.5 cm wide and the length of the perimeter of the balloon. Glue it to the outside rim of the half that will form the base.

To make the feet for the large bowl, cut 3 lengths of the gold-coloured wire, each about 25 cm long. Curl one end of a wire into a snail shape and position the other end against the bowl, bending it so that it follows the shape of the bowl from just below the card rim to the base. Fix the wire in place with a line of glue and small pieces of red paper soaked in wallpaper paste. Repeat with the other 2 lengths of wire, placing them equidistant from each other.

Cover the edges and the part of the legs that are attached to the bowl with more wallpaper paste-coated red paper. Leave to dry.

Decorate the rim of the bowl with the copper-coloured relief pen. Leave to dry.

Attach a decorative bead to the top of the lid with a drop of glue, and add some copper relief motifs.

The small bowl is made in the same way as the large one, but the feet are replaced with a circle of corrugated card, and 2 curled-wire handles are attached to the sides (see opposite).

Christmas

CARDBOARD CHRISTMAS TREE
Size: approximately 1.50 m tall

MATERIALS

2 large recycled cardboard boxes (each at least 1.50 x 1 m) ● Ruler ● Pencil ● Scalpel ● Scissors ● Double-sided tape ● 5 cm-wide gummed kraft paper tape ● Small bowl ● Acrylic paint: 500 ml white, 250 ml mid brown ● 5 cm- and 2 cm-wide paintbrushes.

METHOD

Divide the cardboard into 10 cm squares. Using the templates on pages 120–1, draw the tree shapes using the grid as a guideline. Don't forget to mark the positions for the cardboard wedges.

Cut strips of cardboard about 3 cm wide and to the height of each of the squares marked on the tree shapes. Using double-sided tape, stick them side by side, end on, to one of the tree shapes, in the places indicated, to create wedges and give some thickness to the tree. Stick the duplicate tree on top. Repeat with the other tree shape. Using a scalpel, cut open the slits as shown, adjusting their width to correspond with the thickness of the trees.

To seal the open edges, stick the gummed kraft paper tape around all edges of both trees, including the edges of the slits.

In the small bowl, mix together equal quantities of white and mid-brown acrylic paint and add a small amount of water. Using the wide brush, paint one side of each tree. Leave the trees to dry flat, then turn them over and paint the other side. When they are dry, prop them upright and paint the edges and borders of the shapes with white acrylic paint, using the 2 cm-wide paintbrush.

Slot the 2 tree shapes together.

(see also pages 120–1)

Christmas

FESTIVE WINDOWS

MATERIALS
Large sheet of red card ● Carbon paper ● Ballpoint pen ● Cutting mat ● Scalpel with fine blade ● Newspaper ● Spray glue.

METHOD
Enlarge the templates on page 122 on a photocopier, adjusting the size as necessary to fit your windows. Place the photocopies onto the red card, slide the carbon paper between the 2 layers, then trace over around the shapes using the ballpoint pen.

Place the card onto the cutting mat and, using the scalpel with a fine blade, carefully cut out the shapes. Make sure your windows are clean and dry before mounting your window decorations. Place each decoration on a newspaper-covered surface and spray with the spray glue, then position on the window.

(see also page 122)

Christmas

FEATHERS AND STARS

MOBILE

MATERIALS

White wire ● Wire cutters ● A large assortment of white paper ● Scalpel and/or scissors ● Nylon thread ● Strong glue ● White feathers.

METHOD

Curl a length of wire to form the desired shape of the mobile, starting and finishing with a loop.

Cut a large number of different snowflake shapes from the white papers and attach them to the wire structure either with short lengths of nylon thread or by gluing them directly to the wire. Intersperse the snowflakes with the white feathers, attaching them in the same way. If the snowflakes and feathers are too heavy and cause the wire shape to uncurl, tie the loops of wire together with lengths of nylon thread.

GLASSES

MATERIALS

White sticky-back plastic ● Carbon paper ● Ballpoint pen ● 6 wine glasses ● Scissors.

METHOD

Enlarge the motif below on a photocopier, then lay the pattern onto the paper backing of the sticky-back plastic, slip a sheet of carbon paper between the 2 layers and trace over the motif using the ballpoint pen. Repeat until you have traced 6 motifs.

Cut out the motifs, peel off the paper backing and carefully stick one around the bottom of each wine glass, smoothing out any air bubbles with your fingers before pressing the plastic firmly in place. You can add other smaller motifs above this one, varying them to personalise each glass: hearts, triangles, stars, spots.

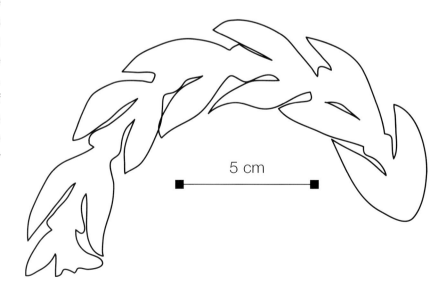

5 cm

Christmas

PRICKED AND EMBOSSED STATIONERY

PRICKED STATIONERY

MATERIALS
Graph paper ● Thin card stock and envelopes ● Corrugated card ● Large pointed needle.

METHOD
Select motifs from a cross-stitch book or design your own on graph paper. (Reduce the design on a photocopier to obtain squares of approximately 3 mm.)
Lay the paper template onto your card stock or envelope, then place both onto the smooth surface of a piece of corrugated card. Using a large pointed needle, prick each square of the motif to transfer it to the paper.

EMBOSSED STATIONERY

MATERIALS
Brass or plastic letter stencils ● Double-sided tape ● Letter or kraft paper and envelopes ● Embossing tool.

METHOD
Fix the stencil in working position on a hard work surface with double-sided tape. Lay your chosen paper over the top, and with the embossing tool, trace around the edges of the shapes, using the fine point for small areas and the large for big areas.
(This is the same technique as used by childen when they place a piece of paper over a coin and draw over the top with a pencil, for example, only here the pencil is replaced with a hard object.)

Christmas

STORYBOOK BOX
Size: 4 x 22.2 x 15 cm

MATERIALS
Metal ruler ● Pencil ● Scalpel ● A3 sheet of 1 mm-thick card ● A3 sheet of 2.4 mm-thick card ● Newspaper ● Spray glue ● Modern Options gold metallic surfacer ● Modern Options patina blue antiquing solution ● Paintbrush ● Carbon paper ● Gold paint ● Scissors ● White corrugated card ● Tea bag ● Glue gun.

METHOD
Cut a rectangle of 37.5 x 22.2 cm from the 1 mm-thick card and 2 rectangles of 22.2 x 14.2 cm from the 2.4 mm-thick card.

Working on a newspaper-covered surface, cover one side of each of the smaller rectangles with spray glue, then lay the large rectangle flat and stick the 2 glued cards at either end as shown on the diagram on page 123 (1).

Paint the whole surface with gold metallic surfacer. Leave to dry for 1 hour, then apply a second coat. While the paint is still tacky, apply the antiquing solution irregularly over the surface using a paintbrush. Leave to dry: the patina effect will become apparent as it dries.

Reduce the template 'Secrets' on page 123 and transfer it to the righthand side of the surface by placing a piece of carbon between the template and the card and tracing over the design. Paint over all parts of the design using the gold paint. Leave to dry.

Turn over (so that 'Secrets' is face down on the left) and paint this surface gold.

Cut 1 strip of 20 x 4 cm and 2 of 15 x 4 cm from the remaining thick card. Round off one end of each of the 2 shorter strips. Using these strips as templates, cut out the same in the corrugated card, positioning the templates so that the grooves run the length of each corrugated-card strip.

Soak the tea bag in a small amount of hot water, allow to cool, then paint the tea over the corrugated card strips to 'age' them. Leave to dry, then stick these strips to the card ones using the spray glue.

Following the diagram on page 123, mark the inside surface of the box form on the righthand side. Using a glue gun, stick the edges of the card strips in position as shown (2). Leave to dry.

Apply glue to the rounded edges. Fold over the 'spine' of the 'book' and stick to the edges. The free part will form the lid of the box.

To simulate a leather binding, cut 4 strips of 9 x 1.5 cm from the remaining 1 mm-thick card. Paint them gold, allow to dry, then glue them around the spine equidistant from each other.

(see also page 123)

Christmas

RICE-PAPER HEARTS

MATERIALS

Rice paper rounds (available from an Asian food store) or wafer paper ● Thin card ● Pencil ● Scalpel ● Scissors ● Hole punch ● Ribbon.

METHOD

Lay a rice paper round onto the card and carefully draw round the edge. Draw a heart in the middle of the card circle and, using the scalpel, cut it out to make a template. Place the heart template onto a rice paper round and draw round the edge with a pencil.

Using the scalpel, make a small cut in the pencil line, large enough to insert the scissors, then carefully cut out the heart. Repeat to obtain several hearts and rounds with hearts removed.

Punch a hole in the top of each shape and thread through a length of ribbon by which to suspend the decoration.

Christmas

WHITE-LEAF MIRROR

MATERIALS

Mirror ● White tissue paper ● Repositionable spray glue ● Scissors ● Pencil ● Cardboard box (optional, see method).

METHOD

Enlarge the templates opposite on a photocopier and transfer them to the tissue paper. Adjust the number and their sizes, or hand-draw your own, depending on the size of your mirror. Cut out the motifs: the thinness of the tissue paper will enable you to cut through several layers at the same time.

Spray the glue onto the back of each motif (ideally spraying outdoors or inside a cardboard box to limit fumes and to prevent glue getting onto other surfaces). Stick the shapes carefully onto the mirror, one at a time, beginning with their stems. To give some relief to the design, cut out the centres of the leaves (shown in grey on the templates) before spraying them with glue, or add a thin strip of paper to the centre of each leaf.

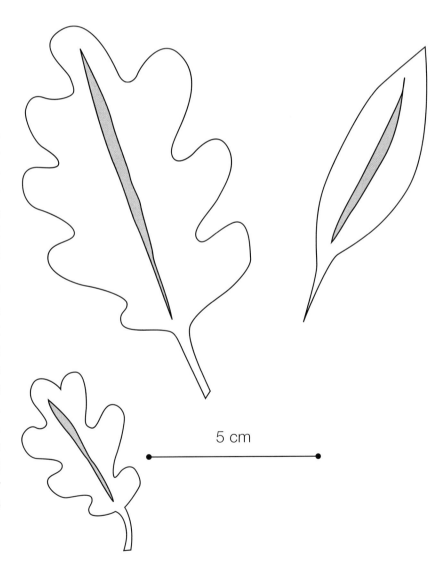

5 cm

Christmas

MANTLEPIECE MAGIC

MATERIALS

Pencil ● Corrugated card ●
Scalpel ● Newspaper ● Spray
paint: copper, gold and silver ●
Double-sided tape ● Red acrylic
paint ● Paintbrush.

METHOD

Draw holly leaves and stars of
different sizes and shapes onto the
smooth surface of the corrugated
card. Vary the position of the motifs
so that the grooves of the card run
in different directions. Cut out the
shapes and remove the central
'vein' from the leaves.

Working on a newspaper-covered
surface, spray the grooved surface
of the shapes with metallic paint.
Leave to dry.

Stick a length of double-sided tape
to the back of each shape, then
stick them around the mantlepiece,
mixing up the shapes, colours and
direction of the grooves.

Paint the smooth side of some
corrugated card with the red acrylic
paint and leave to dry. Cut out
some 'berries' and attach in the
same way between the leaves.

Christmas

LITTLE ANGELS

MATERIALS

Aluminium foil ● Wooden toothpicks ● Tapestry needle ● White feathers (2 for each angel) ● Mini fluted tart tin.

METHOD

Tightly scrunch up a piece of aluminium foil into a ball to form the head and another into a cone shape for the body. Join them together by poking the ends of a wooden toothpick into the 2 parts. To make the arms and legs, tightly roll long, thin sausage shapes from aluminium foil, adding extra to one end of each length to form the hands and feet.

Pierce holes in the body with the large needle and slide the arms and legs into them. Hold in place by scrunching the foil on the body around them. Insert the feathers into the back in the same way.

To make the hat, line the mini fluted tart tin with 2 or 3 layers of aluminium foil, pressing it into all the grooves. Trim the edges. Remove the foil hat from the tray and place it on the angel's head.

Christmas

TEDDY BEARS

PAPIER MÂCHÉ BEAR

MATERIALS
Newspaper ● Gummed kraft paper tape ● Brown and navy blue kraft paper ● Wallpaper paste ● Bowl ● Stiff cardboard ● Scissors ● Raffia ● Needles ● Sewing thread ● 2 buttons ● Felt-tip pens.

METHOD
Crumple sheets of newspaper into a ball for the head. Make a larger ball for the body and 4 sausage shapes for the arms and legs. Assemble these elements using the gummed kraft paper tape to give you the basic form of the bear.

Tear up strips of the kraft paper, keeping the colours separate. Mix up the wallpaper paste in a bowl, following the manufacturer's instructions. Soak the paper in the wallpaper paste and stick the pieces onto the shape, smoothing out air bubbles. Leave the shape to dry overnight in a warm, dry place.

(continues on page 124)

Christmas

PRECIOUS PICTURES

MATERIALS

Metal ruler ● Pencil ● Stiff cardboard ● Cutting mat ● Scalpel ● Newspaper ● White glue ● Glue brush ● Sandpaper ● White acrylic paint ● Paintbrushes ● Coloured inks: jewel colours plus gold.

1. Draw the outlines of the picture frame onto the cardboard. Lay the cardboard onto the cutting mat and cut out the shapes using the scalpel and metal ruler.

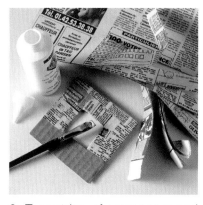

2. Tear strips of newspaper and coat them with the white glue. Stick them to the cardboard frame, covering all surfaces with at least 4 layers of paper. Leave to dry.

3. Sand the frame, then paint with the white acrylic paint. Leave to dry for 2 hours, then sand again. Apply a further 2 coats of paint, allowing each to dry for 2 hours and sanding the frame before applying the next.

4. Paint all surfaces with coloured ink. Leave to dry. Paint the inner and outer edges of the frame with gold ink. Using your finger, apply small touches of gold ink elsewhere on the frame.

Christmas

SILVER BASKETWEAVE BAG
Size: 8 x 14 cm

MATERIALS
Aluminium foil ● White rice paper ● White A4 paper ● Scissors ● Paper glue ● Ruler ● Pencil ● Adhesive tape.

METHOD
Cut 11 strips of 29.7 x 3 cm and 28 strips of 21 x 3 cm from the aluminium foil. Cut 10 strips of 29.7 x 3 cm from the white rice paper. Fold each of the strips in 3 lengthways so that they are each 1 cm wide. Place a sheet of A4 paper vertically on the work surface, then stick the ends of the 29.7 cm-long strips across bottom, using the paper glue, alternating the foil and rice paper strips. Weave the 28 shorter strips of foil over and under between these strips to cover the paper. Glue the loose ends of the strips to the sheet of paper.

On the wrong side of the paper, fold the paper 2.5 cm from each width edge and 8.5 cm from each lengthways edge. Unfold and the paper should look like the diagram on page 125.

Cut along the solid lines to create the gusset. Fold in B, bring together A and C to create the side panels of the bag. Glue the overlapped edges together, allow to dry and then reinforce on the inside with adhesive tape. Repeat for other side.

Cut some strips of aluminium foil and glue them in place inside the bag on either side to form handles.

(see also page 125)

Christmas

LETTERS FROM THE HEART

MATERIALS

Scissors ● White and coloured tracing paper ● Pencil ● Metal ruler.

METHOD

Enlarge the templates (1) to the desired size and, for each heart, cut out 2 shapes in 2 different colours of tracing paper. (Note: the piece between the fold and the end of the cut lines must form a square.) Fold each shape in half as shown. Draw the cut lines onto the shapes, ensuring that all 6 bands (A–F) are the same width. Cut along the lines. Lay the 2 hearts as shown (2) and weave the bands together as follows: slide F closed (i.e. taking the 2 layers together) between the 2 layers of A, then B closed between the 2 layers of F and F closed between the 2 layers of C. Slide A closed between the 2 layers of E, then D closed between the 2 layers of A. Slide E closed between the 2 layers of B, then C closed between the 2 layers of E, B closed between the 2 layers of D, and finally D closed between the 2 layers of C.

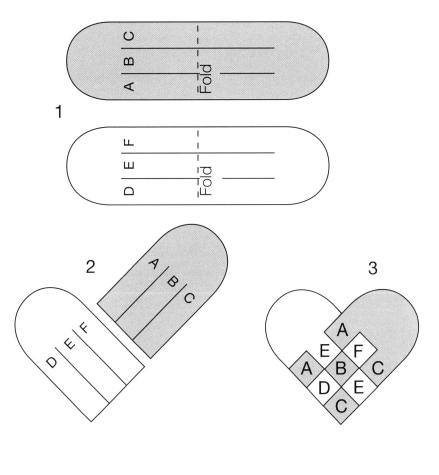

Christmas

WALLPAPER TREE

Size: approximately 2 m tall.

MATERIALS

**1 roll of decorative wallpaper ●
Pencil ● Scissors ● Decorative
paper or paints and paintbrush,
for bauble motifs (optional, see
method) ● Scalpel ● Polystyrene:
7 rectangles of 7 x 3 cm and 2
rectangles of 15 x 3 cm ● Double-
sided tape ● String of fairy lights
● Masking tape.**

METHOD

Draw freehand and then cut out the
4 sections of the Christmas tree:
each should be about 53 cm tall,
and the width of the top of each
section should correspond to the
base of the one above it.

The 'baubles' on the tree shown
opposite are part of the wallpaper
design, If you are unable to find
something similar, use off-cuts from
another decorative paper and stick
them in place on the tree, or simply
paint them onto your chosen paper.
Using the scalpel, cut a small slit in
the centre of each 'bauble'.

Assemble the tree by overlapping
the sections to a greater or lesser
extent depending on the desired
height of the tree. To give some
relief to the tree, stick the
polystyrene rectangles between the
2 layers using double-sided tape
on either side of the block. (Use one
on each side of the base of the top
2 layers, 3 along the base of the
next layer and the 2 long rectangles
at either side of the tree base.)

Beginning at the top of the tree,
slide a fairy light into each hole and
fix in place with a piece of masking
tape on the back.

Make a loop of masking tape and
fix it to the top of the tree, then
suspend it from a hook in the wall.
Alternatively, simply stick the top of
the tree to the wall using double-
sided tape.

Designs and templates

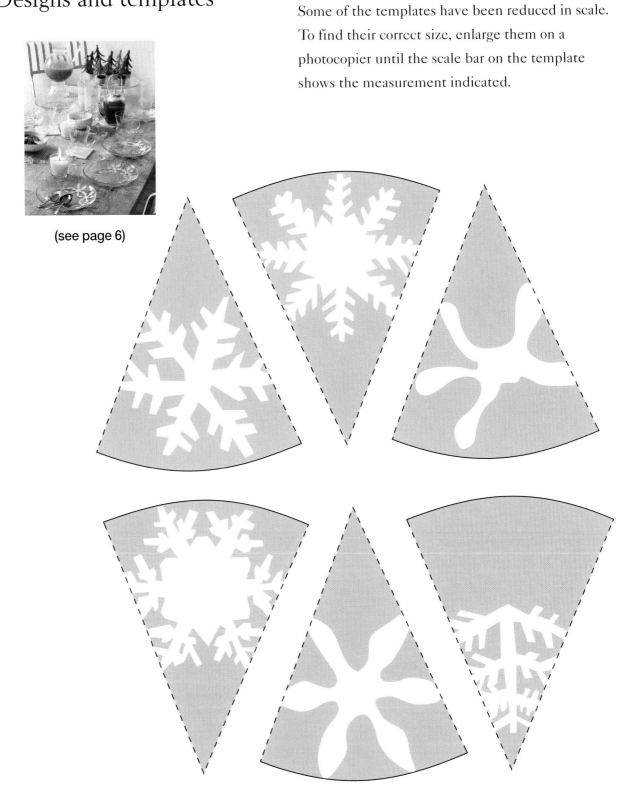

(see page 6)

Some of the templates have been reduced in scale. To find their correct size, enlarge them on a photocopier until the scale bar on the template shows the measurement indicated.

(see page 14)

5 cm

5 cm

Designs and templates

(see page 24)

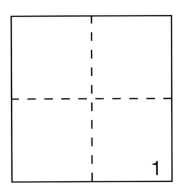

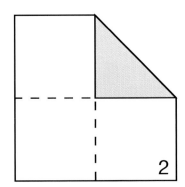

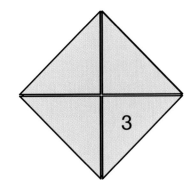

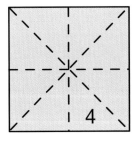

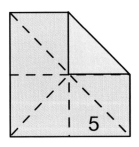

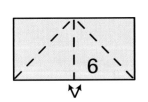

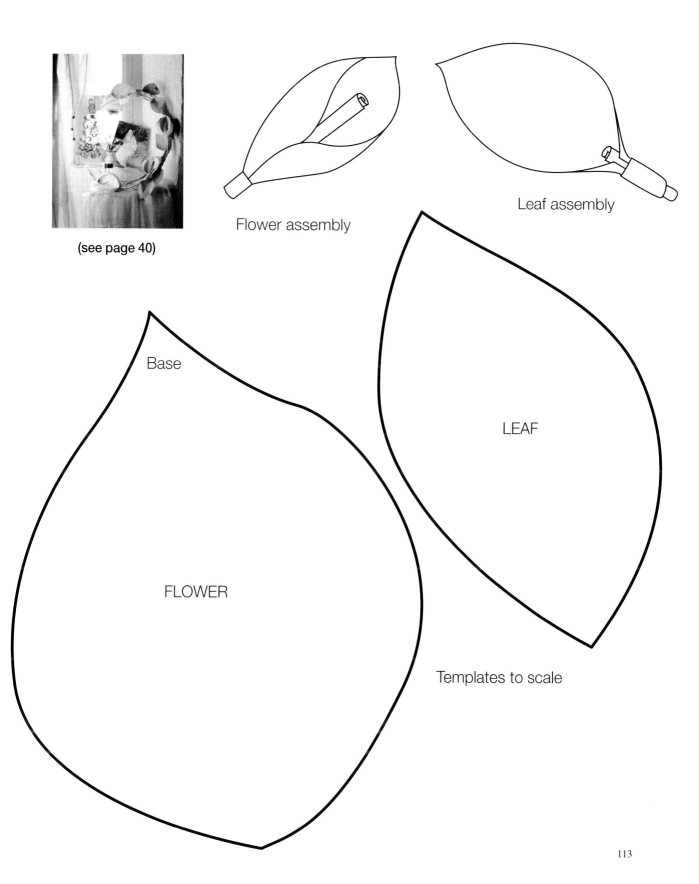

(see page 40)

Flower assembly

Leaf assembly

Base

LEAF

FLOWER

Templates to scale

Designs and templates

(see page 42)

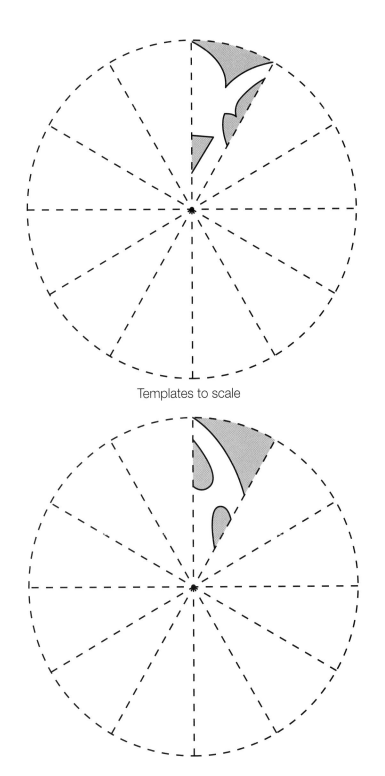

Templates to scale

(see page 44)

Designs and templates

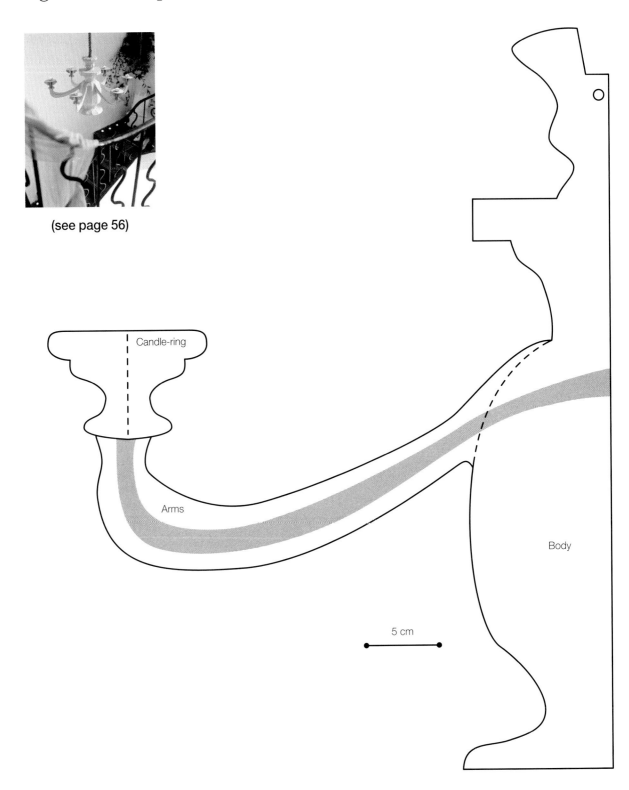

(see page 56)

Candle-ring

Arms

Body

5 cm

(see page 60)

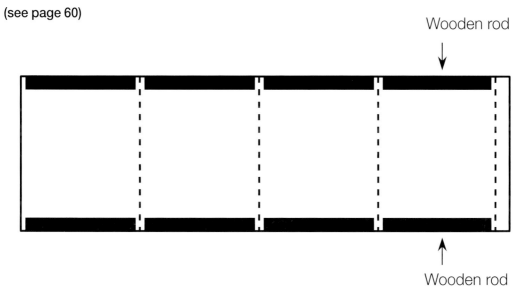

Wooden rod

↓

↑

Wooden rod

20 cm   20 cm   20 cm   20 cm   2 cm

30 cm

Designs and templates

(see page 72)

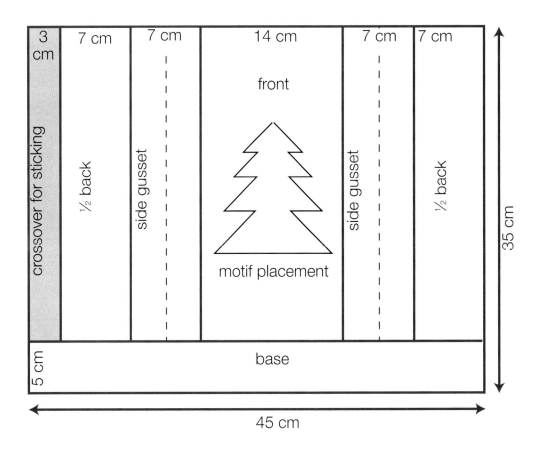

- 3 cm — crossover for sticking
- 5 cm
- 7 cm — ½ back
- 7 cm — side gusset
- 14 cm — front / motif placement
- 7 cm — side gusset
- 7 cm — ½ back
- base
- 35 cm
- 45 cm

Designs and templates

(see page 78)

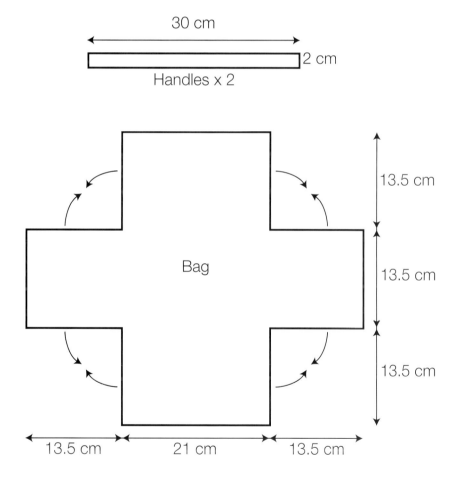

30 cm

2 cm

Handles x 2

Bag

13.5 cm

13.5 cm

13.5 cm

13.5 cm   21 cm   13.5 cm

Designs and templates

(see page 82)

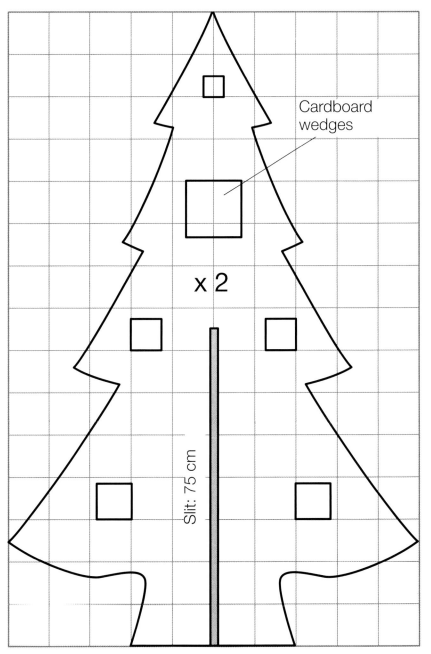

Cardboard wedges

x 2

Slit: 75 cm

1 square = 10 cm^2

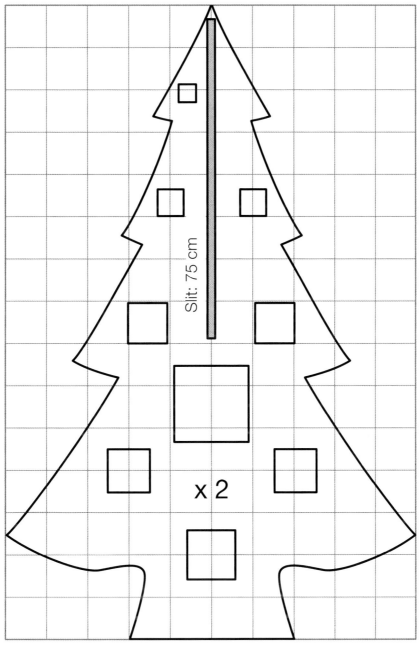

Slit: 75 cm

x 2

1 square = 10 cm²

Designs and templates

(see page 84)

10 cm

10 cm

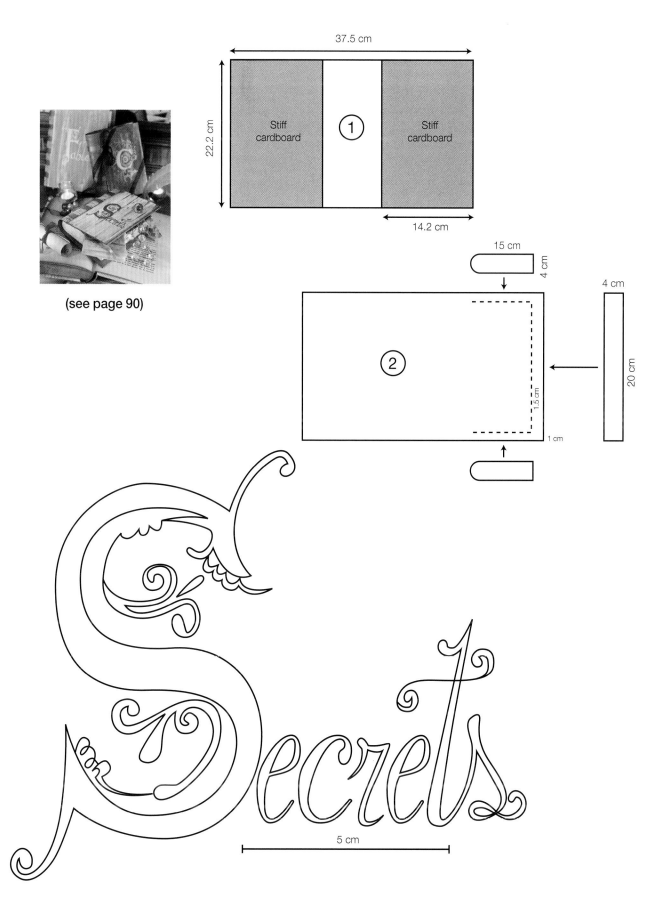

37.5 cm

22.2 cm

Stiff cardboard

①

Stiff cardboard

14.2 cm

(see page 90)

15 cm

4 cm

②

4 cm

20 cm

1.5 cm

1 cm

5 cm

Designs and templates

(continued from page 100)

Rework the form, building it up by adding more paper where needed. When you have achieved the desired shape, cut out the ears from the stiff cardboard. Stick them onto the head with gummed kraft paper tape, then cover them with brown kraft paper coated in the glue. Curve them into shape before they dry. Add a small flattened ball made from crumpled newspaper for the muzzle, fixing it in place with gummed kraft paper.

Cover the whole bear with 6 more layers of glue-soaked paper, the last one brown, allowing each layer to dry before applying the next.

When the bear is completely dry, add the dungarees, using torn strips of glue-coated blue kraft paper. Cut out the shape of the pocket and sew along the edge using the raffia, then stick it in place on the front of the dungarees. Sew a button onto each shoulder strap. Draw on the eyes and snout using the coloured felt-tip pens.

TEDDY BEAR TRAY

MATERIALS
Tray ● Coloured kraft paper: brown, yellow, white, navy blue and pale blue ● Paper glue ● Pencil ● Clear varnish ● Paintbrush.

METHOD
Cover the base of the tray with pieces of glue-coated yellow paper, then form a grid by gluing on thin strips of white paper.

Sketch out the shape of the bears in pencil, then glue pieces of coloured kraft paper in place to fill the design.

When the glue has completely dried, apply a layer of clear varnish over the whole design to protect the surface.

(see page 104)

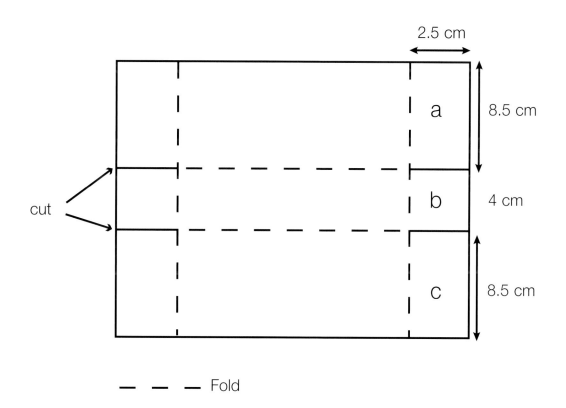

2.5 cm

a — 8.5 cm

b — 4 cm

c — 8.5 cm

cut

— — — Fold

Index

Credits

PHOTOGRAPHERS
Édouard Chauvin (p. 103), Juliette d'Assay (p. 43), Gilles de Chabaneix (pp. 7, 15, 21, 27, 35, 45, 61, 67, 69, 87, 97), Thomas Dhellemmes (pp. 13, 59, 65), Christophe Dugied (pp. 11, 19, 25, 29, 33, 39, 41, 49, 55, 57, 81, 91, 93, 107), Louis Gaillard (pp. 9, 31, 37, 47, 53, 63, 71, 73, 75, 77, 83, 85, 95, 99, 105), Pierre Hussenot (pp. 17, 23, 89), Sylvie Lancrenon (p. 101), Bernard Maltaverne (p. 51), V. Perocheau (p. 109), Frédéric Vasseur (p. 79).

DESIGNERS
Barbro Andersson (p. 107), Marie-France Annasse (p. 13), Nathalie Auzemery (p. 103), Monique Bonnin (pp. 43, 51), Eve-Marie Briolat (pp. 63, 73), Catherine de Chabaneix (pp. 7, 15, 27), Ayako David (p. 67), Ghislaine Descamps (pp. 81, 85, 101), Virginie Desmoulins (pp. 33, 39, 41), Virginie Dillot (pp. 35, 45, 87), Juliette Dupont (p. 47, 59), Céline Dupuy (pp. 25, 77, 83, 95, 109), Marie-Paule Faure (p. 53), Michiru Fujii (pp. 19, 29, 49, 65, 75, 79, 99), Françoise Hamon (pp. 61, 97), Vania Leroy (pp. 9, 11, 55, 71, 91, 105), Véronique Méry (p. 67), Yves Méry (pp. 21, 57), Sonia Richard (p. 23), Évelyne Rouvillois (p. 17), Camille Soulayrol (p. 31), Marion Taslé (pp. 37, 69), Dominique Turbé (p. 93), Laurence Wichegrod (p. 89).

STYLISTS
Ève-Marie Briolat (pp. 63, 73, 109), Pascale Chastres (pp. 23, 31, 89), Catherine de Chabaneix (pp. 21, 35, 45, 61, 67, 69, 87, 97), Virginie Dillot (pp. 7, 15), Christl Exelmans (p. 37), Marie-Paule Faure (p. 53), Marion Faver (pp. 43, 51), Caroline Lancrenon (pp. 23, 89, 101, 103), Vania Leroy (pp. 9, 11, 47, 55, 75, 81, 91, 99, 105), Véronique Méry (p. 27), Camille Soulayrol (pp. 13, 19, 25, 29, 39, 41, 49, 57, 59, 65, 71, 77, 79, 83, 85, 93, 95, 107), Dominique Turbé (pp. 25, 33, 107).